HELPING
YOUR
CHILD
STAY
MORALLY
CLEAN

HELPING YOUR CHILD STAY MORALLY CLEAN

Allan K. Burgess

Deseret Book
Salt Lake City, Utah

ISBN 0-87747-671-3

Library of Congress Catalog Card Number 84-71705

Deseret Book Company

P.O. Box 30178

40 East South Temple

Salt Lake City, Utah 84130

Contents

Introduction

What Successful Parents Are Doing

"My parents help me understand the importance of morality. They always know where I go on dates, who I'm with, and when I'll be home. No going to a girl's house unless her family is home." (Teenage boy.)

I remember walking home from the chapel the night I was called as a bishop. I could see the twinkling lights in the windows of the homes in our ward, and I was overwhelmed with the heavy responsibilities that were now mine. As I struggled under the weight of my new calling, I recalled the promise that the stake president had made to me. He had promised I would receive the help I would need to assist ward members in their spiritual and personal growth. He called this help the mantle of a bishop and told me that it came to all bishops as they worked to fulfill their responsibilities and sought the help of the Lord. The promised help did come, and many times I was inspired to say and do things that changed lives for the better. When I was released seven years later, I felt a definite loss of this mantle and realized that much of any success I had enjoyed came from this help I had received.

Most of us hold a responsibility much more important

than the calling of a bishop. This responsibility is our calling as parents. And as parents, we, too, can have a mantle—extra help from the Lord—to help us teach our children better than any other person or organization. President
Spencer W. Kimball said it this way: "Parents should not
leave the training of children to others. There seems to be a
growing tendency to shift this responsibility from the home
to outside influences such as the school and the church, and
of greater concern, to various child-care agencies and in-
stitutions. Important as these outward influences may be,
they never can adequately take the place of the influence of
the mother and the father. Constant training, constant vig-
ilance, companionship, and being watchmen of our own
children are necessary in order to keep our homes intact and
to bless our children in the Lord's own way." ("Fortify Your
Homes Against Evil," *Ensign*, May 1979, p. 5.)

Righteous, caring, and involved parents can have an
enormous influence for good on their children. A Church
study indicates that "the factor that has by far the greatest
effect on the private religious life of our youth and upon
their achievement of the desired outcomes is home religious
observance. . . . The home and family influence is much
more significant than that exercised by peer groups or by
program participation. In fact, the influence of the home,
whether it be positive or negative, is overwhelming." (Dean
L. Larsen, Regional Representatives Seminar, April 1,
1983.)

Parents need to be especially vigilant in teaching their
children to be morally clean. We cannot afford to leave this
important responsibility to others or to chance.

Many parents are already effectively teaching moral
cleanliness. But when some of them were asked to share
their ideas, most had a difficult time identifying what they
were doing, and some even felt that they were not doing
much at all. Many of their teenagers felt otherwise, how-
ever, and when asked how their parents helped them stay

morally clean, they shared many interesting and worthwhile insights. Here are a few of their responses:

1. By telling me that my body is a temple and that I shouldn't treat it like a visitors' center.

2. Having family night and talking about how it can change your life if you aren't morally clean, and the advantages and blessings you will receive if you are. By being aware of the traps you can get yourself into.

3. They have always expressed the importance of morality and how important a temple marriage is and how being immoral can affect my progress toward this goal. They like me to be in early from dates, and they don't want me to be alone for long periods of time.

4. They themselves have stayed morally clean.

5. By talking to me. By asking me to be around friends who want the same things out of life as I do.

6. My parents help me understand the importance of morality. They always know where I go on dates, who I'm with, and when I'll be home. No going to a girl's house unless her family is home.

7. They discourage me from watching R-rated movies and bad things.

8. By teaching me Church principles and having me pray about them so I know the truth.

9. They have me double date with friends that they know. They encourage me to be active in sports and other hobbies that keep me busy doing other things.

10. By talking to me about the facts of life and making me feel that sex is a special thing.

11. They taught me correct principles at an early age.

12. They brought me up in a good home atmosphere and gave me good restrictions.

13. Lots of small talk.

14. Keeping me from "chasing" with girl friends. Encouraging me to go to church and to stay modest.

15. They tell me how important it is to be married in the

temple. They tell me not to settle for anything less than the best.

16. They don't leave me alone very long when I'm with my girlfriend.

17. Family home evening lessons on the plan of salvation, families are forever, and temple marriage. Use of examples such as family members, friends, famous people, and Bible stories (David, Joseph). Not exposing us to a bad environment (movies, books, bars).

18. They told me never to be in a situation where I would have problems. I wasn't allowed to date until I was sixteen. This gave me time to grow up and make some decisions on my own.

19. They set certain rules that I am expected to abide by.

20. They told me that I would be in big trouble if I did anything of the sort.

21. By talking to me about how important it is to save sex for marriage.

22. They have told me and shown me how important and special it is to be married in the temple, and so I'm going to the temple someday to be as happy as they are.

23. They have taught me that my body is sacred and that I must take care of it.

24. They warned me of single dating and discouraged me from dating non-LDS girls.

25. They have taught me the consequences of facing the Lord for sin and set an example of following the Lord's commandments.

26. My parents have helped me to stay morally clean by teaching the importance of this principle and by showing me how happy their lives are now because of their moral cleanliness which allowed them to have a temple marriage.

27. They have great actions that I follow. They keep immoral things out of the house.

28. Always being there when I need them. Buying only clothes that are morally clean. Talking with me about morality. For my sixteenth birthday my parents bought me a diamond ring and told me that this ring was a promise to them to always do the things they and the Lord wanted me to do.

Another interesting source of information is a study on teenage pregnancy that was directed by the Utah State Office of Education, which commissioned Utah State University to conduct a study comparing sexually active and sexually non-active teenagers in the areas of family relationships, school success, values, and religious background. The results indicate some of the factors that help young people stay morally clean. According to the study, morally clean teenagers:

1. Were more likely to be Latter-day Saints.

2. Had begun dating later.

3. Had more communication with parents, especially with fathers.

4. Felt that their parents' discipline was more consistent.

5. Were more likely to think it was very important to their parents for them to get good grades in school.

6. Were more likely to have plans to go on to college.

7. Attended church more often, currently and two years earlier.

8. Considered themselves to be more religious.

9. Felt more responsible to parents, society, and God for their personal behavior.

10. Were more likely to learn about intercourse from their parents.

11. Were more likely to feel that sex education from parents was adequate.

12. Were less likely to have an unmarried sister who became pregnant.

13. Were more likely to think that petting and intercourse before marriage is wrong.

14. Were less likely to have close friends who had petted and had lost their chastity.

The responses of the teenagers and the results of this study indicate some of the things parents are doing to help their children stay morally clean. The rest of this book will emphasize how we can teach these things to our children.

Each chapter contains ideas that have proven successful in many Latter-day Saint homes and powerful quotations from the General Authorities of the Church. As we learn and practice these ideas and teachings, we will be better able to help our children remain clean and pure and receive the blessings that come from living the law of chastity.

1

Establishing
Spiritual Commitments

"My parents stress temple marriage and the goals that we must have in order to get there. They teach the goals so that they are part of our lives." (Teenage girl.)

When I was five years old, my dad, who was a first-class army cook at the time, made a big pot of homemade vegetable soup. As I smelled it cooking, I decided that I didn't like it even though I hadn't tasted it. When we sat down, I refused to eat the soup, saying that I wanted something else. My father told me that I would not get anything else to eat until I had eaten my soup. I made up my mind that I would never eat that soup—and I got nothing for supper.

When I got up the next morning, my mother made my favorite breakfast and told me that as soon as I ate my soup I could have some. I got nothing for breakfast—or lunch. When dinnertime rolled around, I was mighty hungry, and my mother made a beautiful banana cream pie for dessert. When we sat down to eat, that same ugly bowl of vegetable soup was placed in front of me. Although my dad had been very patient with me up to this time, when I told him that I would starve to death before I ate that vegetable soup, he decided it was time for action. He said I had two choices: I could eat the soup or I could get a spanking and eat the soup. "Either way," he said, "you will eat that soup!"

I chose plan B, which was to get spanked and then eat the soup. After my spanking, I decided that maybe I would try the soup. I took one bite and spit it onto the kitchen floor. My dad took me into the next room, spanked me for spitting, and explained to me that if I spit again, he would spank me again. With this kind of creative reasoning going on, I decided that I would eat my soup. And I did—about three spoonfuls, with help from my dad.

I then got to eat a delicious supper and to have a huge piece of banana cream pie. I have always liked banana cream pie, but it was years before I ate vegetable soup again. Now I eat it all the time because I want to.

It is always easier to get a person to do something if he wants to do it. If we really want our children to keep high dating standards and stay morally clean, we need to help them want to do so as much as we want them to. This will never happen unless they share some of the spiritual insights that we feel. Until then, we may face the same uphill battle that my father faced with the vegetable soup. But once our children establish their own strong spiritual commitments, the battle is two-thirds won.

The Church recently completed a study among young men twelve to eighteen years old. The study attempted to determine what factors have the greatest influence upon the worthiness of a young man to receive the Melchizedek Priesthood, serve a mission, and marry in the temple.

The study considered the importance of public and private religious behavior in the lives of young men. Public religious performance is participation in meetings and activities. Private religious behavior deals with experiences not measured on correlated reports, such as personal scripture study and private prayer. The study reported the following:

The involvement of young men in public religious performance is much heavier than it is in the private religious experiences in their lives. This discrepancy between public religious performance and the involvement in private religious experience is of tremendous importance in determining whether or not the youth achieve the desired outcomes in their lives. The study among young men disclosed that private religious behavior is much more powerful in this regard than is public performance. This finding tells us something of great importance about where we should be placing emphasis. If we communicate to our young people that their participation in meetings and activities is the most essential part of their religious lives, and they do not feel of our constant concern for the influences that work in their private religious experience, then we will not be as effective as we should be in helping them achieve the ultimate objectives. It would appear from the findings in the recent study that our youth are presently under the general impression that what matters most is their participation in the public religious performances. If this is true to any degree, we have a reason for bringing this emphasis into better balance. This is one of the things we can do to make a difference in the outcomes." (Dean L. Larsen, Regional Representatives Seminar, April 1, 1983.)

One thing, then, that will help us help our children stay morally clean is to emphasize their personal spiritual growth. As they grow spiritually they will be more inclined to keep the right moral standards and make correct decisions. As Elder Larsen indicates, spiritual growth deals with more than just church attendance: "Every effort should be made to encourage the young men and young women to attend seminary, Sunday School, Aaronic Priesthood quorum meetings and activities, and Young Women's classes. But keep in mind that such attendance is not an end in itself. Activity in these programs is no guarantee of movement toward the most important goals. It must be supportive of what happens at home and [of] the personal influence of adult leaders whose relationship to the young people can be of such great importance." (Ibid.)

The study found that the most powerful factors in helping young men live worthily, advance in the priesthood, serve missions, and marry in the temple were:

1. A home life that includes regular family prayer, gospel study, and agreement on basic values.

2. Private religious behavior, such as personal prayer and personal study of the scriptures.

3. A strong personal relationship with a trusted, admired adult adviser.

4. Program participation that reinforces the above three things.

To strengthen our children, we can emphasize the importance of the scriptures in our own lives and make them one of our family priorities. The study found that "if a young person lives in a home situation where there is regular family prayer, regular family study of the gospel and the scriptures, and agreement on basic values, the likelihood of his going on a mission and being married in the temple is greatly enhanced." Example is so important in all phases of spiritual growth.

Here are a few comments from teenagers on how their parents taught them through example the importance of chastity:

1. *We don't watch any immoral television shows, and we are advised to choose music and friends wisely.*

2. *They have made us want to become like them. We see how happy the gospel makes them and that it is the only way that we can be really happy for eternity.*

3. *They had me read President Kimball's book* The Miracle of Forgiveness.

4. *They talk with clean conversation and dress modestly.*

5. *They never go to R-rated movies, and they wear the right type of clothes.*

6. *They set a good example in their church callings.*

7. *They stress temple marriage and the goals that we must have in order to get there. They teach the goals so that they are part of our lives.*

We need to encourage our children to become involved

in personal scripture study and help them to have meaning-ful personal prayers. Here are a few ways to do this:

1. Use special events to emphasize the scriptures and personal prayer. For example, we can give our children their own scriptures (now available at very modest prices). We can help our seven-year-olds mark scriptures about baptism, and we can discuss these scriptures with them. Before our sons turn sixteen, we can have them mark the sacrament prayers in their scriptures and encourage them to memorize the prayers. We can teach our children to pray before dates, baptisms, ordinations, and other events. Once we have done this, a reminder is usually all it will take to keep them praying.

2. Allow children to read the scriptures for fifteen min-utes after their bedtime. This will be time well spent.

3. Center home evenings around the scriptures and have each member of the family mark at least one scripture each week.

4. Obtain a list of the missionary scriptures and learn them as a family.

5. Spend a home evening looking up scriptures about prayer and make a list of things that we can do to have more meaningful prayers.

6. Make sure that each child has regular opportunities to pray vocally in the family.

7. Emphasize that we attend church to learn how to live, and that we need to live what we learn in order to grow spiritually. A quotation that most children will remember is "Sitting in church doesn't make us a Christian any more than sleeping in a garage makes us a car."

All of these ideas are intended to help children *want* to stay morally clean. No motivation is stronger than a per-sonal testimony that comes from study, prayer, and living the gospel. Once our children have a testimony of the gos-pel and its moral standards, they will want to work with us to establish guidelines to help them stay morally clean.

2

Teaching Modesty and the Sanctity of the Body

"They have taught me from the time I was little that my body is a temple and that I should always keep it modest and clean." (Teenage girl.)

Most of us have reverent feelings when we discuss or enter one of the temples. Most young people share these same feelings, and we can use these feelings to teach them that the most important temple is their own body. They can come to understand that when they swear, attend inappropriate entertainment, dress immodestly, or neck and pet, they are doing these things in a holy temple—their body. There are three great principles to help teach the sanctity of the body: (1) The body is a temple, (2) we can dedicate ourselves, and (3) modesty is important.

The Body Is a Temple

Doctrine and Covenants 93:35 and 1 Corinthians 3: 16-17 are excellent passages that teach that the body is a temple. We can ask our children to list the things that they feel would be inappropriate to do in a temple. Then we can read these two scriptural passages and discuss the fact that our bodies are actually more important and eternal temples than any building made of brick or stone. Finally, we can have our children see how many things on their list would be wrong to do in their bodies. They will find that nearly all of the things that they listed as wrong to do in a "build-ing" temple are also wrong to do in a "body" temple. This exercise can establish powerful guidelines for future be-havior. We might want to conclude our discussion with the following quotation:

> Your spirit, which is a child of God and lives eternally, will pos-sess your present body forever. What kind of a body or temple do you want your spirit to live in throughout the eternities of time? When the time of resurrection comes, you cannot take out of the grave a different body than the one placed in it. . . .
>
> Our bodies are temples of God. We should not think of entering one of the temples of our God and desecrating His holy house. The temple of the body which houses a spirit child of God is far more important to Him than brick or mortar, for has he not said that his work and glory is to bring to pass the immortality and the Eternal Life of man? (Delbert L. Stapley, *How to Resist Temptation* [Salt Lake City, Utah: The Church of Jesus Christ of Latter-day Saints, 1974], pp. 20, 21-22.)

We Can Dedicate Ourselves

We had the special opportunity of attending the dedica-tion of the Jordan River Temple with our children. Our two boys, even though they were fairly young, sat quietly for four hours without saying one word. They were very im-pressed with the sacredness of the temple.

When temples and chapels are dedicated, they are turned over to the Lord for his purposes. Through our day-to-day living, we can do the same with our bodies. We might teach this principle to our children by describing a building dedication that we have attended and then asking them what it means to dedicate a building to the Lord. We could than suggest that we can do something similiar with our personal temples—our bodies. We can promise the Lord that we will keep our bodies clean and pure and dedicate our time and talents to the Lord. By keeping our bodies clean they become, like temples of stone, places where the Lord's

Spirit can dwell. At the dedication of the Spanish Fork Seminary building on August 29, 1962, Elder Boyd K. Packer said:

> In dedicating a building, we present it officially as our gift to the Lord. . . . We are then under serious responsibility to maintain the building as beautiful and appealing as it can be made. We are under responsibility to have a spirit here in the building that is completely worthy of the ownership of the building; and we are under the necessity of maintaining order among the students in such a way that there will be no disrespect either in conduct, thought, or action toward the purpose for which this building was erected.

We can draw at least three ideas from this quotation to help teach our children. We can dedicate ourselves to the Lord by:

1. Dressing and taking care of our bodies in a beautiful, appealing way.

2. Living so that the Lord's Spirit can dwell with us.

3. Showing respect for ourselves and the Lord through our conduct, thoughts, and actions.

Modesty Is Important

We should start while our children are young to teach them the importance of modesty. This will help them to realize that their body is special and sacred. One thing we can do is avoid dressing our children in halter tops, immodest swimsuits, sunsuits, and other apparel that is inappropriate for an adult to wear. If our children never start dressing immodestly, they will never have to change bad habits.

Some of the specific styles of dress that we should avoid have been discussed in the *New Era*:

> 1. Bathing suit styles. There was a time when a one-piece suit was modest and appropriate for LDS girls. Now even these can be extremely revealing and should be chosen carefully. There are now immodest styles for young men, too.
> 2. Sun dresses are a popular mode of apparel this year, and some LDS girls are wearing dresses with only straps covering their

shoulders, which is inappropriate. Some young ladies are even wearing such dresses to Church dances and meetings.

3. Many of the T-shirts worn by both boys and girls flaunt suggestive or vulgar writing on the front or back.

4. Halter tops and shorts are being worn to school and other public places. Cutoffs are often too cut off.

5. Rather than supporting church standards, young priesthood holders sometimes encourage girl friends and sisters to dress in the immodest fashions of the day. (Carol J. Wood, "It's Your Ball Game," *New Era*, June 1978, p. 10.)

As we teach our children that they should always keep their bodies properly covered, we should also teach them that modesty goes much deeper than just the clothes they wear. President N. Eldon Tanner has said, "Modesty in dress is a quality of mind and heart, born of respect for oneself, one's fellowmen, and the creator of us all. Modesty reflects an attitude of humility, decency and propriety. Consistent with these principles and guided by the Holy Spirit, let parents, teachers, and youth discuss the particulars of dress, grooming, and personal appearance." ("Friend to Friend," *The Friend*, June 1971, p. 3.)

Modesty reflects the way we feel about the Lord and ourselves. As we teach our children the gospel and help them gain their own testimonies, their desire to dress modestly will increase. An excellent example of this principle was a young man we will call Chuck. At age nineteen, Chuck had done just about everything wrong that a nineteen-year-old was capable of doing, and he looked and dressed the part. He had, among other things, the wildest hair imaginable, and his clothing was extremely casual and dirty. One day, Chuck went in to see his bishop and told him that he wanted to change and become active in the Church. He started to attend his meetings, and as he grew spiritually, an interesting thing happened: his appearance and dress started to improve. One Sunday morning when he attended church, it was difficult to recognize him. He had cut off about twenty pounds of hair and was wearing a suit and tie.

His bishop congratulated him on his appearance. Chuck told the bishop that he had felt uncomfortable about his dress and hair and had decided to clean up and look like a representative of the Lord.

About six weeks later, he made another dramatic change by showing up with a missionary haircut and a smile from ear to ear. He was going to baptize a friend and didn't feel comfortable about using the priesthood if he didn't look his best. The Spirit was teaching Chuck how he should look and dress.

We can teach our children that every one of us has a perfect guide to fashion and style. It is not Paris, fashion magazines, or peers, but the Holy Ghost. Our children need to know that the Lord cares more about modesty and good grooming than he does about fashion, and that it's not the name on our shoes or jeans that counts but how we wear and carry the name of the Lord. We can teach them the importance of listening to the Holy Ghost and asking the Lord what is appropriate to wear.

Following are comments from teenagers explaining what their parents have done to help them dress modestly and feel that their bodies are sacred:

1. *They bought me clothes and helped me dress properly when I was younger, and I have stayed with the same habits of modest dress.*

2. *They have always taught me how special my body is.*

3. *They go with me when I buy my school clothes and help me pick out what is appropriate to wear.*

4. *They have told me all of my life that I look better covered up.*

5. *They have pointed out scriptures that show my body is a temple and shouldn't be handled by anyone before I am married.*

6. *They have taught me to wear clothes that I feel comfortable in and to cover the parts of my body that should be covered.*

7. *They dress modestly themselves.*

8. *They have taught me that I can buy clothes that are in*

style but still modest and that I should never wear clothes that put ideas in people's heads.

    9. *By dressing me modestly from the time I was a child and explaining that no one should see my body.*

    10. *They have taught me self-respect and helped me feel good about myself.*

    11. *They explain why they want me to dress modestly—because my body is sacred.*

    12. *They have taught me from the time I was little that my body is a temple and that I should always keep it modest and clean.*

    13. *Ever since I was small my parents have always taught me to dress modestly and to try and behave the same way.*

3

Teaching About Sex and Its Sanctity

"I just kind of figured things out as I went along. My cousin told me most of it in a kind of silly way. Once my dad asked me if I knew, and I told him yes. He said nothing else, but I always wished that he would have told me himself." (Teenage boy.)

Teenagers have indicated that less than 10 percent of them were taught the facts of life by their parents. The rest of them learned about this sacred power of procreation from other sources. These included:

1. School and health classes.
2. Television and movies.
3. Books and magazines.
4. Friends and other relatives.
5. Dirty jokes and "gutter talk."
6. Special programs.
7. "On the street."

Elder Mark E. Petersen indicated the real problem with such teaching when he said that "the proper teaching of sex requires also the teaching of complete chastity . . . to do otherwise is nothing less than suicidal." (*Conference Report*, April 5, 1969, p. 63.)

Parents Can Teach It Best

Sex education really does belong in the home where it can be taught in a sensitive and proper way throughout the growing years of our children. Elder Petersen taught, "Sex education belongs in the home, where parents can teach chastity in a spiritual environment as they reveal the facts of life to their children. There, in all plainness, the youngsters can be taught that procreation is a part of the creative work of God and that, therefore, the act of replenishing the earth must be kept on the high plane of personal purity that God provides, free from all forms of perversion. *Unskilled parents can learn to teach their children properly.* In fact, God commands it, and who are we to disobey?" (*Conference Report,* April 1969, p. 64; italics added.)

Terrance and Marvia Drake explain why parents can teach their children about reproduction and chastity better than anyone else:

> There are several reasons parents are best suited to teach their children about sexuality. The first is availability. No other person spends more time with a child than the child's mother and father. Thus, parents can teach when questions first come up. No other people share with children the intimacy of such events as bath time, potty training, menstruation, and so on. Prepared parents sensitive to the process of teaching about sexuality are far superior to a schoolteacher exposed to children for only a few hours in a formal setting.
>
> Also, parents share with their children common values and love and concern. Sexuality cannot and should not be separated from morality. No one is better qualified to teach chastity, self-control, and moral conduct than parents. As parents answer their children's earliest questions about sexuality or childbirth, they can emphasize the sacred nature of reproduction and the body. (Terrance S. Drake, M.D., and Marvia Brown Drake, *Teaching Your Child about Sex* [Salt Lake City: Deseret Book Co., 1983], p. 5.)

Most bookstores have many aids to help parents teach this critical and sensitive subject, although these should be used only with great care, as some do not agree with our values. The greatest aid of all is the Holy Ghost. If we prepare ourselves and seek the Spirit, we will know when the times are right for teaching and what to say.

As a father recently contemplated teaching one of his sons, he found himself very nervous, but their talk was much easier and more rewarding than he had expected. He had prepared himself and prayed for a good opportunity to talk to his son. One day, when they were alone, his son asked a question that was the perfect lead-in to a discussion. Because the father was prepared, they had a good talk together. Since that day, they have had many other worthwhile discussions on the subject.

As our children mature, we should have several personal discussions with them, not just one. In fact, teaching about sex and morality is a process that begins when our children are young and continues until they leave home. Some things, such as necking, petting, masturbation, and homosexuality, are sensitive areas, but each needs to be discussed at the appropriate time. Through study, planning, and prayer, we can prepare ourselves with the information that we will need. When common sense and the Spirit indicate that the time is right, we will then be able to fulfill this important and rewarding responsibility.

Following are comments from teenagers who responded to these questions: "Did your parents teach you the facts of life? If yes, what did they do that was helpful and effective? If no, where did you learn the facts of life?"

1. *Yes and no! Some things they told me and some I learned from others.*

2. *They talked to me and gave me a book written by an LDS doctor.*

3. *No. I learned at school by talking with my married cousin, at health class, and from friends.*

4. *I learned at a school presentation I attended with my mother. After the program, she answered any questions that I had.*

5. *My parents taught me that sex was very sacred and*

shouldn't be done out of wedlock.

6. Yes, they were open with me and told me all that I needed to know and asked me to be open with them.

7. No, not really, because when they decided it was time to tell me I had already learned all that I needed to know from listening to others.

8. No, I just learned from friends whose parents told them.

9. Yes, they told me everything so that I would not misunderstand anything or be confused.

10. No, they didn't teach me anything. I just kind of picked up on it at school. It wasn't too hard. It's an often-mentioned topic.

11. My dad really helped; he made it so that I could understand it.

12. Yes, they came right out and talked about it and didn't beat around the bush.

13. Yes, we have a small farm and have private talks where I can ask any question.

14. I feel that my parents just threw a few facts at me. My cousins and family members helped more.

15. I learned the basic procedure of sex from friends, literature, etc. My parents did teach me how, when, where, with whom, and in what frame of mind to be in.

16. Yes, they taught me according to the gospel and how it all related—like when it is good and when it is bad and what is good or bad.

17. They have taught me to do everything with my Heavenly Father's help.

18. No, I learned from dirty jokes, street language, and other students in the sixth grade.

19. No, I just accumulated knowledge through the years.

20. Yes, my parents gave me some literature from the Church that told me the importance of the subject.

21. Yes, the main thing that my parents did was make a book with pictures of families, babies, cartoons, husbands and wives, and other things that deal somewhat affectionately with the sub-

ject. (*They did this to ease the pressure.*) Then there was some written information that dealt with the spiritual side and explained our calling to be married and have children. After that came all the details.

22. No, I learned it from gutter talk. My parents told me absolutely nothing and won't talk about it unless I bring it up. They act like they're scared to tell me, and they are appalled when they find out the things that I know.

23. No, I learned most of it from friends or on TV shows, but it would be better if my parents had told me.

24. No, I learned from my brother and from books, and I am learning more from friends all the time.

25. Yes, I asked my mother questions and that is how I learned about it.

26. Yes and no. They just explained what they thought I should know and told me to try and not be tempted. I also learned from the streets, but I wish my parents and I talked about it more.

4

Developing Communication

"My parents have made it so we can talk to them like they're our best friends, and they've shown that they really care about us." *(Teenage girl.)*

The relationship between parents and teenagers is critical. Studies show that a good father-daughter relationship is one of the leading contributors to moral cleanliness. Many girls that have become pregnant out of wedlock have sought companionship with a boy because they did not receive the love and affection that they needed from their fathers. A good relationship begins long before adolescence but must especially be nurtured through the teen years. These do not need to be years of isolation and conflict between parents and teens; they can be rewarding and enjoyable for both. Here are some suggestions for making them that way.

Have Fun Together

Start while your children are young to hold family home evening. Make it enjoyable and learn to do things together. Develop a tradition of Sundays and Mondays together as a family. If we plan enjoyable activities, our teenagers will continue to want to do things with our families. These activities do not need to be complicated or expensive. Here are some Sunday afternoon activities that most families will enjoy.

1. Design, make, and deliver a family award to someone special in your ward or neighborhood.

2. Have a talent show. Each member of the family can do something, no matter how young or untalented they feel they are.

3. Have a testimony meeting after fast and testimony meeting for those who didn't share their testimonies at church.

4. If you have small children, have a penny hike. If you flip heads you turn right, and if you flip tails you turn left. Look for interesting things that show how wonderful our world is.

5. Write letters to grandparents or other family members.

6. Play a religious game.

7. Sing Church hymns and songs.

8. Tell stories from the scriptures and follow them up with related crossword puzzles, word searches, or other fun ways to apply the story. Older teenagers will enjoy making the puzzles or searches.

9. Play gospel review games. *Zonkers and Other Games for Latter-Day Saint Homes and Classrooms,* by Allan K. Burgess and Max H. Molgard, contains twenty-five review games and six hundred gospel questions.

10. Spend a few minutes together writing in your journals. A journal for younger children could be kept by older children or by the parents.

Develop Similar Interests

We should develop hobbies teenagers might enjoy, such as tennis, basketball, crafts, carpentry, camping, fishing, stamp collecting, cooking, or music. With a little thought and research, we can find many interests to share with our children throughout their teenage years.

Show Support

We should support our children in their school, Church, and community activities and compliment them on their achievements. When we attend sports events, music recitals, or other activities in which our children participate, we should look for positive things to say even if our child is not a first-string player or star of the activity. Here are some examples of things to say:

1. You didn't make one bad pass the whole game.
2. You read your part perfectly.
3. I was watching you, and you sang every song.
4. As you played the piano I was proud of the dignity and poise that you showed.
5. You talked loud enough so that everyone could hear.

Hold Personal Interviews

Fathers should hold personal interviews monthly with each child. We should pick a good day, such as Fast Sunday, and hold them regularly, being sure to include things our children want to discuss. In these interviews, we can find out some of the things that are bothering them and informally interview them about how they are living the gospel. These are good times to bear our testimonies to our children and have them bear theirs. We can find out how they feel about the gospel, their Church leaders and teachers, friends, school, and other members of the family. If the father cannot or will not hold these interviews, they could be held by the mother.

We need to be careful to keep our questions and comments positive and friendly. This is a time to build closeness, not a time to discipline. Here are some questions that might get interviews started on a positive note:

1. What do you enjoy most about our family?
2. Where do we go as a family that you enjoy most?
3. When was the last time I told you that I loved you? I would like to tell you today.
4. Which Church teacher do you like the best? Why?

5. Do you know any people that you feel will go to the celestial kingdom? Why do you feel they are going there?

Notice that these questions give us an opportunity to move into a gospel or family discussion where we can talk about personal things without prying or sounding like we are conducting a criminal investigation.

The following two quotations from young people demonstrate two problems that we need to avoid during these interviews:

> I have a pretty good level of communication with my parents. We don't often argue, but when we do, we settle our differences fairly easily. But there's one thing I never talk to my parents about. When I do something wrong, I'd like to be able to go to my parents and say "Look, I've done this and I'm really sorry I did. What can I do to repair the damage?"
>
> But I can't do that. I'm so afraid I'll disappoint my parents' faith in me, and I end up getting a new, long version of an old lecture instead of the advice and sympathy I need. So I go to a friend or a teacher and ask their advice, and then try to settle it on my own. And I usually come out OK. But I really wish I had enough faith in myself and in my parents' trust to admit my errors to them. If I were sure my parents could love and respect me, in spite of mistakes, I'd be even more confident that my Father in heaven could do the same." (Fifteen-year-old girl, "Parents, Are You Listening?" *Ensign*, Feb. 1971, p. 54.)

> I often found it difficult to talk over problems with my father, but this was not always the case. For there was no problem when we saw eye to eye on the solution. But the problem arose when I knew that the answer that my father would give me would be in opposition to my own views. It would anger him if I decided to act on my own decision, if it opposed his. For this reason I would only consult with him about a problem if I knew we would both be thinking along the same lines. (Twenty-year-old boy, Ibid., p. 56.)

Be a Good Example

Teenagers notice a phony in a hurry. We need to be careful about asking them to do something that we are not willing to do. We should not expect their language, choice of entertainment, or Church activity to be on a higher plain than our own.

Interact with Your Children

Being home is not enough. Sitting together watching television will not accomplish what we desire. We need to interact with our children. A study completed in 1975 turned up some very interesting information about fathers: "The study found that those fathers who were at home had the same effect on their children as those fathers who were gone in the service, dead, or divorced—unless they were interacting with the children. In other words, if a father isn't talking with his children, working with them, playing with them, listening to them—according to this research, he does not really influence them." ("Fathers—Present and Absent," *Ensign*, June 1980, p. 11; see D. Russell Crane, "Father Absence and Male Sex-Role Development," *Family Perspective*, Winter 1978, pp. 35-40.)

This interaction should be positive. The relationship we are seeking is built through trust and friendship, not criticism and doubt.

Establish Proper Roles

Our children need to see proper male and female roles in their parents. If they have strong, loving, understanding, religious parents, they will tend to look for these traits in those whom they date and marry. Probably the realization that their parents really love each other is one of the greatest gifts parents can ever give their children.

Use Authority Properly

We should try to show our children common courtesy and respect. The Lord has told us the principles we should follow in all our relationships:

> No power or influence can or ought to be maintained by virtue of the priesthood, only by persuasion, by long-suffering, by gentleness and meekness, and by love unfeigned; by kindness, and pure knowledge, which shall greatly enlarge the soul without hypocrisy, and without guile— reproving betimes [i.e., early] with sharpness, when moved upon by the Holy Ghost; and then showing forth

afterwards an increase of love toward him whom thou hast re-
proved, lest he esteem thee to be his enemy; that he may know that
thy faithfulness is stronger than the cords of death. (D&C 121:41-
44.)

When we follow this counsel, we develop mutual respect, trust, and love that cannot be developed in any other
way.

Express Love

We can look for ways to express and demonstrate our
love for our children. It doesn't mean much if we love our
children but they don't know it. Our relationship is
strengthened when we demonstrate our love by both our
words and our actions. And as we build our children, we
also build our relationship with them. Here are some examples of how a parent might verbally express love:

1. As I watched you pass the sacrament today I was so
proud of you. You always dress properly and pass the sacrament with such dignity and reverence. I'm sure that
Heavenly Father is proud of you too.

2. When you offered to do your sister's dishes last night
so she could go with her friends, it made me so happy.

3. Your little brother told me that you took him to the
park yesterday. I know that he really loves you for it, and I
love you too.

4. Thanks for making your bed before you went to
school this morning. You sure make my job a lot easier
when you take care of your own things.

5. Did you know that I love you just for being you?

Spend the Time

Many busy parents stress the importance of spending
"quality time" with children. But spending *lots* of quality
time is also very important. President Spencer W. Kimball
has suggested the following:

> We all realize that communication is a two-way street, and that
> youth often build their own barriers. But are parents charting their

course right in this matter? Mothers, are you so busy with social life, with clubs, with working out of the home, or with housework, that you have no time to sit down and talk to your little girls and tell them the things they should know when they are nine, and ten, and eleven, and older? Can you be frank and loving to them so that they in turn can be frank in giving you their confidences?

And you fathers, are you so busy making a living, playing golf, bowling, hunting, that you do not have time to talk to your boys and hold them close to you and win their confidence? Or do you brush them off, so that they dare not come and talk about these things with you? (*The Miracle of Forgiveness* [Salt Lake City: Book-craft, 1969], p. 258.)

Listen

One of the most important things we can ever do is just take the time to listen to our children. Dr. Brent Barlow told an interesting story in the *Deseret News* about communicating with children:

> Recently Brian, who is a seventh grader, told me that something was bothering him and he wanted to talk to me alone. We agreed to do it that evening and all during the day I was proud that one of my sons would confide in me during a father-and-son talk.
>
> Later that night, after everyone else had gone to bed, Brian and I met for our talk. "It has been on my mind for some time now and I wanted to ask you a question." I leaned back in my chair and tried to look fatherly. "And what is your question, Brian?"
>
> "I've been wondering," he began, "if you stood on your head and ate a sandwich, would the food go up or down?" I thanked Brian for confiding in me and after a few moments of silence I told him that I did not know the answer. But true to my training in family counseling, I suggested that perhaps we could seek the answer together.
>
> Brian asked if one of us could do an experiment and I said perhaps so. He then said he was tired and wanted to go to bed. If I did decide to stand on my head and eat a sandwich, he said to let him know in the morning. (*Deseret News*, December 15, 1983, p. C2.)

Many times our children will want to talk with us about things that we feel are not very important, as in this story. But because Dr. Barlow listened and showed interest, his son is more apt to talk with him about more serious things as they come along. Many children actually start out a serious discussion with a light question. If we show interest and really listen, they then follow up with what is really bothering them. It is important to listen not only with our ears but with our bodies also. Eye contact, facial expressions, and other body language help build confidence that we really are interested. Our communication as a family will greatly increase as we concentrate on talking less and listening more. Following are comments from teenagers about how their parents help them feel that they can talk to them about personal problems:

1. *They sit down with me once in a while and share very personal parts of their lives with me.*

2. *My mother and I talk about everything, and she is always telling me that if I have a problem I can talk to her.*

3. *They are always there for me. They are never too busy to talk with me.*

4. *They can sense when I am having a problem, and they will come to me and ask me if I need someone to talk to.*

5. *They treat me as a friend, and they come to me with their problems.*

6. *They let me know that they are concerned, and they just allow me to talk to them freely.*

7. *They talked to me about their problems and told me that I could talk to them if I ever had a problem. They said that they would even love me more if I asked them for help with my problems.*

8. *My parents are always ready to listen to and advise me concerning any problem, but they don't try to pry into my life. They let me come to them, and, because of this, I feel more comfortable in coming to them.*

9. *They show me they care for me, and we have personal interviews often.*

10. *They have made it so we can talk to them like they're our best friends, and they've shown that they really care about us.*

11. *By being open with me and just coming right out and saying that they will always be there for me, whenever I need them.*

12. *They listen, try to understand how I feel, and explain things to me that I don't understand.*

13. *We would always do things and share things as a family. My mom, especially, can tell when I have had a bad day, and she is always there for me.*

14. *We talk about our daydreams and fantasies, the things that mean a lot to us—and that helps us to be able to relax with them and tell them our problems.*

15. *They trust me and know that I will tell them everything.*

16. *They won't get mad, and I feel they will understand.*

17. *By being a friend rather than a judge. By telling me personal things of their own and bringing me to their level in confidential matters.*

18. *They ask me about school, and they don't criticize me for things I've done. They encourage me to do my best.*

19. *They have personal interviews with me every Fast Sunday and always show interest in my activities and schoolwork.*

20. *They seem to understand and know what I'm going through and realize how I feel. They are willing to listen.*

5

Dealing with
Early and Steady Dating

"My parents helped me not date until I was sixteen, and they encourage me to double date until I'm eighteen. They expect me to tell them where I am going and when I'll be home, and then to be home on time." (Teenage boy.)

A few years ago a meeting was held with a person who was working with LDS teenagers who had become unwed mothers. He led a very enlightening discussion and one of the questions asked of him was "What had he found to be some of the leading causes of immorality in the lives of the young women that he had worked with?" He said that the three major causes of immorality that he had come in contact with were *early dating, steady dating, and a poor relationship between the girl and her father.* This seems to correlate with the minimum standards that President Kimball gave when he said:

> "Any dating or pairing off in social contacts should be postponed until at least the age of 16 or older, and even then there should still be much judgment used in selections and in the seriousness. Young people should still limit the close contacts for several years, since the boy will be going on his mission when he is 19 years old.
>
> Dating and especially steady dating in the early teens is most

hazardous. It distorts the whole picture of life . . . I hope fervently that I am making clear the position of the Lord and his church on these . . . practices." ("President Kimball Speaks Out on Morality," *New Era*, Nov. 1980, p. 42.)

As parents, we do need to consider the seriousness of early and steady dating. This is especially true with the immorality that faces young people today. Specific dating guidelines give teenagers time to prepare themselves emotionally and spiritually *before* they are placed in difficult moral situations that take a lot of self-control and maturity. President Kimball has indicated the good effect that keeping these standards could have on the youth of the Church: "It is my considered feeling, having had some experience in interviewing youth, that the change of this one pattern of social activities of our youth would immediately eliminate a majority of the sins of our young folks; would preclude numerous early, forced marriages; would greatly reduce school dropouts; and would be most influential in bringing a great majority of our young men and women to the holy marriage altar at the temple—clean, sweet, full of faith to become the worthy parents of the next generation. ("Save the Youth of Zion," *Improvement Era*, Sept. 1965, p. 806.)

Because early and steady dating is so widespread and acceptable, even among some Church members, it is not always easy to help our children maintain these standards. Here are some ideas that may be helpful.

Start Young

It is very important that we discuss dating standards while our children are young and before they become emotionally involved with a person of the opposite sex. The difficulty of overcoming emotional involvement is illustrated by the story of a company that wanted to market rattlesnake meat. They knew of the negative feelings that most people would have toward rattlesnake meat. In order to overcome this emotional involvement, they decided to have a special banquet and invite community leaders and their wives. They did not indicate what the main course was going to be—just that they were establishing a new industry in the community and wanted to get the support of community leaders.

Because the community wanted to encourage new industry, a large group turned out for the special banquet. Naturally, the main course was rattlesnake, and it made quite a hit with the guests. They loved it, and most of them were very curious about what it could be. One guest said that it tasted like pork; another diagnosed it as some kind of chicken.

Just before dessert was served, one of the hosts asked for everyone's attention. He said that they were going to market the delicious meat that had just been served and he hoped that everyone would support their company in its new endeavor. He then announced that they had all just eaten and thoroughly enjoyed rattlesnake meat.

The whole crowd went into an uproar, and the company personnel felt lucky just to get away with their lives. Some of the guests even looked into the possibility of suing the company for feeding them rattlesnake meat under false pretenses.

The story demonstrates how difficult it is to teach people once they are emotionally involved. It underscores the importance of teaching our children dating and moral standards while they are young. President Kimball has suggested that parents "chart and guide the course of their children's lives in the early years. Then there will be none of the intimacies that spell sin and ruin." (*The Miracle of Forgiveness*, p. 257.)

Many families play lots of review games, and by the time their children are five or six years old the parents are asking them questions like "How old do you need to be before you date?" and "When should you consider going steady?" Through constant review from the time they are young, we can help our children make the decision to keep the dating standards of the Church.

As our children grow older, and before emotional involvement sets in, we may want to do and teach some of the following things:

1. Ask our children how they feel about the Prophet and share with them our testimony of him. As they come to realize that he really is a prophet, his teachings will become more important to them.

2. Make attractive copies of President Kimball's statement on dating, frame them, and give one to each child to hang in his or her room.

3. Read with our children President Kimball's statement and other quotations on dating from other General Authorities and bear our testimony that the prophets speak for the Lord. One sister who did this said that her children, who were all in their teens, committed to keeping these standards after just reading what the prophets had asked them to do.

4. Teach our children that keeping Church dating standards will help them spiritually. Help them realize that the Lord has given them these dating standards for their benefit and that they really can't accept President Kimball as a prophet and at the same time reject what he has said.

5. Help our children set their own dating goals and guidelines that are in harmony with the teachings of the Church. They might share their goals with us and the Lord.

6. Encourage our children to promise the Lord that they will keep Church dating standards. They can also ask the Lord for his help in doing so.

7. Have our children record their goals in their journals. If they waver when they become emotionally involved, reading their own journals may help them to remember what their real goals and desires are.

8. Encourage our children to gain a personal testimony of Church dating standards. A personal confirmation from the Holy Ghost is one of the strongest motivations that our

children will ever receive. We can teach them the steps they can follow to gain this personal witness.

Use Real-Life Situations

As friends and acquaintances of our children are forced into early marriages, in a kind and nonjudgmental manner we can help our children see that they don't want to get into the same situation. We can point out the relationship between early and steady dating and the present situation of their friends. Many teenagers say that this approach is very effective.

This approach can be damaging if not used properly, but when used with sensitivity and the guidance of the Spirit, it can be very effective. We need to make sure that we do not criticize, condemn, or stand in judgment of others. Our children need to feel the love and compassion that we have for their friends and feel our concern that they don't suffer the same problems.

One teenage girl had a close friend who became a wife and a mother at age fourteen. As the girl's parents discussed the situation with her, their hearts went out to her friend, and they discussed how her early and steady dating had led to her present situation.

During their conversation, the daughter asked, "Dad, why didn't her parents tell her that she couldn't date?" She added, "You know, kids don't always know what is best for them."

This discussion about dating standards helped the daughter become more firm in her desire to follow the counsel of the prophets.

Use Positive Peer Pressure

In recent surveys, teenagers were asked who they felt had the most influence in their lives; their most frequent answer was friends. Being accepted by their peers is the number-one concern of many teenagers.

Because early and steady dating is accepted and in many

places expected, this pressure from friends becomes a real challenge that parents need to deal with. One comment I have heard over and over again from young people is, "I'm the only one who is not dating before I'm sixteen!" What the teenager is really saying is "I don't know another person who is trying to keep these dating standards, and I feel all alone."

We can help our children know of other teenagers who have the same goals and standards as they do. If we don't know of any, we can check with Church leaders, seminary teachers, parents, friends, and other young people. Then when our children say, "I am the only one who isn't dating yet!" we can say, "What about Bill, and Sally, and Fred, and Mary, and Mark?" If some of these teenagers live in other areas, our children might enjoy writing to them about their common goals and interests.

One step better would be for our children and some of their friends to make a pact with each other that they will keep Church dating standards and support each other in their goals.

Last year in our community we started an organization called P.A.L.S. (People Against Low Standards). In order to join P.A.L.S. a teenager needed to be willing to not date until age sixteen, not steady date, not indulge in parking or other inappropriate dating activities, and have clean language. The organization started with forty young people signing up; within three months it had grown to over eighty members. Many of these young people wanted to keep Church dating standards and were looking for a way they could do so and still be accepted by their peers. We should never underestimate the power of peer influence.

If Everything Else Fails, Kindly Say No!

President Kimball has taught, "Young parents should chart a course in their home and family life which will give the children firm but loving guidance and not let the children rule in the home." (*Miracle of Forgiveness*, p. 256.)

The ideal would be to be able to teach our children correct dating principles and then let them govern themselves. But after we have taught our children and they still want to engage in early or steady dating, we need to kindly and lovingly but firmly say no. Most children will not rebel if we have established a warm and loving relationship with them. It may even be better for them to rebel a little and suffer a guilty conscience than to have our permission to do something that is contrary to the counsel of the Church. If we lovingly and kindly say no, there will come a time when most of our children will thank us for our leadership.

One bishop noticed a trend with those who had suffered serious moral difficulties. He said without exception they had all engaged in early dating, steady dating, frequent steady dating, and staying out late at night on their dates.

I will always be grateful to the father of a girl who lived in my ward when I was younger. When I was sixteen, with the help of a friend, I got up enough courage to ask this girl for a date. Her name was Cindy. My friend dialed her number for me. Cindy answered the phone, and I asked her if she would like to go to the movie with me. At first she didn't say anything; then she said that, if I would wait a minute, she would ask her dad.

I could hear their voices in the background but I couldn't hear what they were saying. Finally Cindy's father came to the phone. He said, "Allan, don't you know that you aren't supposed to date until you're sixteen?" I told him that I was sixteen. He said that his daughter wasn't sixteen and wanted to know why I was asking her out. I really didn't have a good answer, but it didn't matter because he started to talk again. He said, "Why don't you call back in two years and we'll talk about it."

Since that day I have thought a lot about what Cindy's father said. He really loved his daughter and wanted what was best for her. It is the same with our Heavenly Father. He cares for us and our children enough that he has given guidelines to ensure our safety and happiness.

6

Establishing Dating Standards

"I should be home at eleven-thirty. I should make sure I always have a dime, and if something happens I am to call home. If my date wants to do something immoral, I'm to tell him to call my dad. If my dad says it's okay, then it's okay. (My dad is very strong in the Church.)" (Teenage girl.)

Teenagers want to be clean and pure. They want to marry in the temple. Most of them know what is best for them—at least until they become emotionally involved. This was indicated recently when seminary students were asked two interesting questions. The first question was, "If you were a parent and had a fifteen-year-old son or daughter, what would you do to ensure that he or she stayed morally clean?" Here are the most frequent responses:

1. *I wouldn't let them date until they were sixteen.*
2. *I wouldn't let them steady date.*
3. *I would make them be home at an early hour.*
4. *I would hold personal interviews with them.*
5. *I would teach them the importance of chastity.*
6. *I wouldn't let them go to R-rated movies.*
7. *I would set a good example for them.*
8. *I would teach them while they were young.*

9. *I would keep them involved in church.*
10. *I would listen to them.*
11. *I would encourage double dating.*
12. *I would teach them that their body is a temple.*
13. *I would show them that I love them.*

The second question was, "Your future mate is probably dating someone right now. How do you want him or her to handle the dating years?" The students gave very conservative answers, and almost all of them gave the same answers:

I want my future mate during his or her dating years to:

1. *Be in by midnight at the latest or just a few minutes after the activity is over. (Some said their future mate should be in by ten o'clock.)*
2. *Only double date.*
3. *Never go further than a good-night kiss.*
4. *Not date until sixteen.*
5. *Definitely never go steady.*
6. *Never park.*

These answers demonstrate that most teenagers really do know what is best for them. But they need our help. As a matter of fact, although they don't always act like it, they *want* our help. They face some temptations that are stronger and more subtle than they are prepared to handle. We need to work with our teenagers in establishing rules and guidelines that will help them stay morally clean. The rules we establish need to be reasonable ones that really do fulfill a needed purpose. Here are some rules that young people indicated have helped them:

1. *Don't stay in the car anywhere.*
2. *Date a wide variety of people.*
3. *Double date and group date.*
4. *Parents have to meet dates and talk with them.*
5. *Date LDS people with same values.*
6. *Go to planned activities.*
7. *Be home at a definite time.*
8. *Date someone of a similar age.*

9. *Never be alone with a date at a home.*
10. *Don't date until age sixteen.*
11. *Can't own a personal car but can use the family car.*
12. *Pray alone and with parents before dates.*
13. *Set guidelines on kissing.*
14. *Cannot date on school nights—only on weekends.*
15. *Date other people between dates with a boyfriend or girlfriend.*

As we establish our own family rules, we should discuss them with our children and try to share with them the reasons for each rule. They may not totally understand or agree, but they can feel our concern and know that we are establishing the rules to help them reach their spiritual goals.

Sometimes rules can give our children an excuse to use with their friends and on dates that will help them save face and still do what is right. One girl has arranged a signal with her mother, and when she doesn't want to go somewhere, she flashes this signal. If a boy calls on the phone and she doesn't want to date him, her mother will yell out, "You're not going anywhere—you've been gone too much already!" The boy thinks the mother is a real dragon, but the girl is off the hook. If her friends come by and ask her to go someplace questionable, she flashes the signal and her mother steps in.

Established rules can also give our children a good excuse for avoiding bad situations. They can say that their parents have a rule that they must be in by eleven o'clock or that they are not allowed to date until they are sixteen. This allows them to save face with their friends and helps them avoid the powerful influence of social pressure.

Although some teenagers argue about dating guidelines, indications are that most teenagers appreciate them, even if they don't always show it.

The following responses from teenagers can give us numerous ideas for worthwhile dating guidelines. Notice how positive the teenagers are about their family rules. You can almost feel their gratitude as they share their feelings. They are responding to the question "What are some of the dating guidelines your parents have established that have helped you stay morally clean?"

1. *They ask me before every date, "Where are you going?" I am supposed to reply, "The celestial kingdom!"*

2. *They act like they trust me. They set a curfew, are interested in the who, where, how, and what of my dates, and let me use the family car.*

3. *They didn't let me date until I was sixteen, and I am to bring the girl home in the same shape that I took her out.*

4. *Be home by a certain time, never be alone with your date in a car or home, no low-lit lights. Be with others as much as you can and not be alone so much.*

5. *They make sure that they meet the guy before I go out and make sure that I know that he is to treat me right, and I make sure that he does.*

6. *Be in by twelve o'clock. Don't kiss a guy on the first date. Be selective about who you date and where you are going.*

7. *Do not date guys too far out of my age range.*

8. *Date LDS people, those with the same values. Have planned activities, not including parking. Don't stay out after midnight unless it's a special occasion like a dance. Just hold hands as long as possible.*

9. *I have to double date, and my mother always talks to my dates before we go out. She lets them know that she expects them to show respect for me and me the same with them.*

10. *I should be home at eleven-thirty. I should make sure I always have a dime, and if something happens I am to call home. If my date wants to do something immoral, I'm to tell him to call my dad. If my dad says it's okay, then it's okay. (My dad is very strong in the Church.)*

11. *Treat the girl like you would want your mother or sister to be treated.*

12. *Wait until sixteen to date and always double date.*

13. *Date one night during the week and once on the weekend.*

14. *Be home about twelve o'clock, dress modestly, date Church members, go on group dates, and know something about the guy and his reputation.*

15. *Choose friends wisely and date the people I would marry.*

16. *Date in groups with friends. Report to both parents what we are doing and when we will be back. Be back before one o'clock. (That means the girl is home by twelve-thirty.) Be a gentleman and mind my manners. Be happy and enjoy ourselves while on the date. (Boredom can lead to trouble.) Respect our dates and those we are with.*

17. *Weekend dating only. Can't see boyfriend on school nights.*

18. *I must tell my parents what I am going to do and when I will be home, and I must call them if I make any changes in my plans.*

19. *I need to be in by twelve o'clock, not date older guys, and my parents need to meet my date.*

20. *Always pray before going on a date. My parents have told me that I don't have to kiss the guy for anything.*

21. *Don't stay in the car anywhere (driveway, parking lot, streetside, etc.). Midnight curfew. Date a wide variety of girls, not just one. Don't get too intimate. Don't try something thinking that you know when to stop.*

7

Helping in the Choice of Friends

"If my parents feel that I am associating with the wrong people, they ask me to spend less time with those people and more time with others that are more suitable. They let me know that they trust me but don't always trust my friends." (Teenage boy.)

While our children are young we should teach them to choose friends who will help them live the gospel. This will later help them select suitable dating companions. Trying to help children select good friends is a sensitive matter and must be handled with patience and understanding, not ultimatums and commands. Following are some ideas for helping children choose good friends.

Teach Children What a Good Friend Is

Our children could more easily choose good friends if they knew what a good friend is. Elder Marvin J. Ashton teaches that good friends care enough for us that they want to make us better: "There seems to be a misunderstanding on the part of some men today as to what it means to be a friend. Acts of a friend should result in self-improvement, better attitudes, self-reliance, comfort, consolation, self-respect, and better welfare. Certainly the word *friend* is misused if it is identified with a person who contributes to our delinquency, misery, and heartaches. When we make a man feel he is wanted, his whole attitude changes. Our friendship will be recognizable if our actions and attitudes result in improvement and independence." (*Conference Report*, Oct. 1972, p. 32.)

Once our children learn that a good friend is one who tries to make them better, they are in a position to make wise decisions concerning their friends. The following checklist can be used to help evaluate friends.

1. If I slept over at my friend's house, I would feel comfortable kneeling down and saying my prayers.

2. My friend doesn't ask me to do things that are wrong.

3. I usually feel happy and positive when I'm with my friend.

4. My friend uses good language and helps me want to do the same.

5. My friend would return change if given too much at the store.

6. I notice that I act better when I'm with my friend.

7. My friend sneaks around and does things that his parents don't want him to.

8. My friend thinks everything is stupid and puts everyone down.

9. My friend never goes to church and makes fun of my religious feelings.

10. I usually don't feel comfortable inside when I'm with my friend.

Help Children Avoid Bad Friends

Children need to understand that it is not because they are too good for people that we want them to be selective. It is because they may not be strong enough to do the things that are right when they are with certain friends. Elder Neal A. Maxwell put it this way: "Do not company with fornicators—not because you are too good for them but, as

Lewis wrote, because you are not good enough. Remember that bad situations can wear down even good people. Joseph had both good sense and good legs in fleeing from Potiphar's wife." ("The Stern but Sweet Seventh Commandment," *New Era*, June 1979, p. 42.)

We need to let our children know that the Church asks us all to avoid those who would be a bad influence. Young people are not the only ones who can be swayed by friends. Few people of any age are strong enough to associate with poor company and not compromise their beliefs. Here are some examples that we might share with our children:

1. Bishops and other Church leaders, as strong as they are, have received instructions that they should not travel alone or meet too often alone with a person of the opposite sex. They are not to put themselves into a position where they might be tempted.

2. Potiphar's wife wanted Joseph to be immoral with her. Joseph not only told her no but actually ran from the house. Through his actions he taught us that we should get as far as possible from those who might tempt us. (See Genesis 39:7-12.)

3. The apostle Paul taught that we should avoid even the appearance of evil. (1 Thessalonians 5:22.) It is dangerous to see how close we can get to sin without actually sinning. We need good friends who will help us avoid sin as much as possible.

4. One of the major reasons for Solomon's downfall was that he married the wrong person and she influenced him to do wrong. (See 1 Kings 11:1-13.)

Our children may feel better about being asked to evaluate their own friends as they come to realize that all of us are striving to do the same thing.

Build Friendships at Home

Almost all of us need to feel accepted. Some young people choose poor friends because they don't receive the acceptance that they need at home. If we can help our children feel warmth, friendship, and acceptance at home, their need to be accepted by others will be diminished. Then they can become more selective in their friendships. Here are some suggestions that will help us become better friends with our children:

1. Listen. As a person confides in another, their friendship grows.

2. Share time with them. It takes time to build a relationship.

3. Give positive and sincere praise. Both parties feel good when praise is given.

4. Show interest in the things they are doing.

5. Accept them as they are and help them grow.

6. Recognize that they have feelings and desires and let them have their way when possible.

7. Try to understand them, not judge them. Discuss problems before making snap decisions.

8. Confide in them. They will feel important and closer to us as we trust them and invite them into our lives.

Relax and Give Love and Support

Most of us had great fantasies as teenagers and would sometimes imagine ourselves as star athletes, cheerleaders, or sterling scholars. Very few of us had these fantasies fulfilled, but we still seemed to develop into fairly successful parents and Church members. We need to be careful to avoid trying to relive some of these teenage fantasies through our children. We want them to be well-liked and successful, but we need to be careful not to push them too hard. President Kimball discusses this problem: "The mother who thinks it cute to permit her little girl makeup, high heels, or fancy hairdos is asking for trouble. Those parents who permit or encourage early social activities are unwittingly begging for sorrows and heartbreaks. Mothers often fear spinsterhood for their teenage daughters who are not immediately popular. Their every push is likely to bring them sorrows and tears." (*Improvement Era*, Sept. 1965, p. 763.)

Sometimes our teenagers share feelings of discouragement with us when they fail to get dates, are rejected, lose elections, or don't seem to have many friends. It is difficult for us not to feel discouraged along with them and, in some cases, overreact to the problem. A large percentage of teenagers never hold a high-school office, never become extremely popular, or don't even date while in high school, yet they become happily married and successful adults. We need to relax a little during these years and just give our children plenty of love and support. These feelings of frustration and discouragement are just part of growing up.

Following are comments from teenagers on how to help them choose good friends:

1. *My parents encourage me to have good friends and then do things together with us, like take us water skiing.*

2. *They tell me that I should select friends that have the same standards as mine so there will be no temptation.*

3. *They influence us to choose worthy friends—ones we can look up to and who will set a good example for us. They then trust us to choose only the best.*

4. *They put great emphasis on my friends and like to know what they are like and what their influence is on me. They express their feelings about them, but they don't choose them for me.*

5. *By telling me what they expect from me and expressing that friends should want the same things I want out of life. Also by being an example and choosing proper friends themselves.*

6. *They tell me to choose good friends because my friends will be like my future spouse.*

7. *They want to meet our friends, and they let them know that they love us.*

8. *They teach us right from wrong and the value of good friends.*

9. *I tell my parents about my friends and they help me decide.*

10. *They help me to know what qualities to look for in a friend and what a real friend is.*

11. *They ask me about all of my friends and their backgrounds. They encourage me to hang around with the best ones possible.*

12. *By choosing to live in a community where they felt there were good neighbors and the Church was an important part of the neighborhood.*

13. *My parents have told me of their experiences with their friends when they were my age and usually let me know how they feel about my friends.*

14. *They don't select my friends unless they get the feeling that they are not the right people for me to hang around with. Then we talk about it and come to a decision.*

15. *If they feel that I am associating with the wrong people, they ask me to spend less time with those people and more time with others that are more suitable. They let me know that they trust me but don't always trust my friends.*

16. *They ask me if I feel good with the friends that I have. They ask me if I want to be like the friends that I have.*

8

Teaching the Importance of Chastity

"When you keep the law of chastity, it helps you try harder because you know that you can make it to the celestial kingdom. If you don't, you feel like it's an unreachable goal." (Teenage girl.)

A serious attitude problem that some teenagers have today is shown well in the following letter that was received by Elder Thomas S. Monson: "When I joined [the Church], I was engaged to a wonderful man who had left for the service three months prior to my becoming a member. He has since returned, and I spent Christmas vacation with him. Brother Monson, I broke the Word of Wisdom. I was guilty of doubting the teachings of the Church, and I slept with the boy I love several times. I don't in the least regret or feel ashamed of having shared my love with him, but I truly am ashamed of having taken a taste of rum and Coke." (*Pathways to Perfection* [Salt Lake City: Deseret Book Co., 1974], p. 88.)

It is doubtful that most teenagers in the Church feel that chastity is not important, but our children do need support against the barrage of material that suggests that immorality is acceptable. This chapter contains ideas that may be helpful in emphasizing the importance of chastity.

55

Study the Principle of Chastity

Chapter five in President Spencer W. Kimball's book *The Miracle of Forgiveness* contains excellent information on the seriousness of immorality. It would be good to study this chapter and then teach some of the concepts that President Kimball stresses. As our children get older, we could encourage them to read this chapter for themselves. They could also read other information on the seriousness of immorality.

Teach the Consequences of Immorality

Even in this life, certain consequences follow immorality, and many of these take place whether we repent or not. These consequences are not inflicted upon us by God but come naturally because of our actions. Some of the consequences do not follow every immoral act, but no disobedient person can avoid all of them. As young people realize the consequences of immoral behavior, they become more committed to the moral law.

As part of a recent family home evening, one family generated a list of the possible consequences of immorality. Here is their list. We might share this list with our children or have them generate a list of their own:

1. Loss of the guidance of the Holy Ghost. The Spirit cannot dwell in an unclean tabernacle.

2. Pregnancy and the problem of being unprepared to handle the responsibilities of parenthood. Along with this are the problems created for a baby born into a home to parents who don't have the maturity, training, or resources to take care of the baby properly.

3. Early marriage to a person they may or may not love or be able to live with and the loss of freedom to choose the person they really want to marry.

4. Loss of self-respect. A person can never do what is wrong and still completely like himself.

5. Loss of respect from others.

6. Loss of educational and vocational opportunities.

7. Pain and heartache for all who care about the couple—family, friends, and Church leaders.

8. Loss of gospel opportunities such as temple marriage and serving a full-time mission.

9. Venereal diseases.

10. Abortion.

11. Emotional problems. The boy and girl are never sure that their mate really loves them and wants to be married to them. Distrust is also a problem because they haven't been chaste in the past.

12. Emotional problems for the child, who may feel that he or she is not wanted by the parents.

13. Teenage parents don't really fit in socially with other teens or with adults and face some serious social adjustments.

14. Because of embarrassment or feelings of unworthiness, many young people drop out of church and find it very difficult to return.

Teach the Blessings of Chastity

In the long run, positive feelings are more motivating than negative ones. Studies indicate that reward changes behavior much more readily than does punishment. Generating a list with our family of the blessings that accompany chastity can be a worthwhile activity. Here is such a list that one family generated:

1. Worthy to go to the temple and serve in the church.

2. A clear conscience.

3. A better self-image.

4. A stronger possibility of attracting someone with high ideals and good character traits.

5. The companionship and guidance of the Holy Ghost.

6. Greater opportunities to counsel our own children after marriage, and they can better look to us as an example.

7. Better possibilities for a good education.

8. Master of our own destiny instead of circumstances dictating what our future may be.

9. Avoid venereal diseases.

10. Opportunity to choose our mate.

11. A future marriage built on trust and respect.

12. Respected and admired by others, which places us in a position where we can better help others.

13. Both our Heavenly and earthly parents will be proud of us and feel a sense of joy and satisfaction.

No One Can Sin and Get Away with It

The people after the time of Noah built a tower that they said would "reach unto heaven." (Genesis 11:4.) Their purpose seems to have been to build a tower so high that they could sin and then when God caused another flood, they could climb up above the flood and mock God. They really felt that they could sin and get away with it. This seems to be a prevalent attitude today, and we may want to remind our children that no one can sin and get away with it. President Spencer W. Kimball has said, "There comes a time when the fornicator, like the murderer, wishes he could hide—hide from all the world, from all the ghosts, and especially his own, but there is no place to hide. There are dark corners and hidden spots and closed cars in which the transgression can be committed, but to totally conceal it is impossible. There is no night so dark, no room so tightly locked, no canyon so closed in, no desert so totally uninhabited that one can find a place to hide from his sins, from himself, or from the Lord. Eventually, one must face the great Maker. (*The Teachings of Spencer W. Kimball* [Salt Lake City: Bookcraft, 1982], pp. 265-66.)

Our children can come to understand and remember that there are always at least three people who know what is happening on a date—the boy, the girl, and the Lord. They can be taught how pleased and happy Heavenly Father feels when they date properly and keep themselves clean and pure.

Teach Chastity Often

Because of the constant barrage of propaganda that supports and promotes immorality, we could make moral cleanliness a regular agenda item in our family home evenings. It is much more effective to consistently discuss different aspects of morality than to dump the whole load one Sunday afternoon and then not bring it up again for a year or two. It is also very important to use a variety of approaches and avoid preaching. Some of the ideas in chapter six may help.

Choose Uplifting Entertainment

Elder Boyd K. Packer has written, "His devilish invitations appear on billboards. They are coined into jokes and written into the lyrics of songs. They are acted out on television and at theaters. They will stare at you now from most magazines. There are magazines—you know the word, pornography—open, wicked persuasions to pervert and misuse this sacred power. You grow up in a society where before you is the constant invitation to tamper with these sacred powers." (*Conference Report*, Apr. 1972, p. 138)

In spite of everything that we say to our children, they notice what we do and where we go. They pay attention to what we watch on television and which movies we decide to make part of our lives.

It will be much easier to teach our children the sacredness and importance of chastity if we choose entertainment that does not include suggestive or immoral material.

As a matter of fact, one of the greatest teaching tools that we have is our selection of books, magazines, and entertainment. Following are comments from teenagers about the blessings that come from keeping the law of chastity:

1. *At one time in my life I started to go down the wrong path. I went back and repented. When I did this it seemed like I had more friends and better friends. I became a lot happier in life and everything just worked better for me.*

2. *You can marry who you want and who you love in the*

temple and be with them forever. You will be free from guilt. You will be free to choose an occupation you want—rather than be forced to find a job to support an accidental family. You remain free to choose what you want.

3. You have good self-esteem. Peace is more prevalent in the home. It is easier to excel in school and other activities. You are happy.

4. You can just feel good about yourself, and you are able to have a temple marriage.

5. I will be able to find the person I want to marry and who I want to be with for the rest of my life.

6. I don't become a father, so I have the blessing of only having to support one person on my part-time job.

7. Self-confidence, self-power, integrity.

8. Eternal life, accompaniment of the Lord's Spirit, and a clear conscience.

9. Better life and a good reputation.

10. You feel worthy and clean inside.

11. You have freedom to choose.

12. You don't feel cheap and used but feel good about yourself.

13. You can be married in the temple and have the priesthood in your home.

14. During chastity lessons in church I feel a strong spiritual feeling inside, and I see how happy my parents are because they were married in the temple.

15. It will keep your family closer together.

16. You are much happier and you have a special glow about you. One day it will help you to meet a nice guy and marry him.

17. Your parents trust you if they know that you are morally clean and do the right things.

18. A temple marriage and a good reputation.

19. Good conscience. You don't feel that someone is always about to tell others what you have done.

20. The biggest blessing is that you can go through the temple with your chosen mate with no guilty feelings.

9

Helping Children
Who Have Transgressed

"Parents should talk to them. They probably have problems and feel like their parents don't care about them. Parents should calmly talk to them and understand how they feel. They should let them know that they care and want to help." (Teenage boy.)

There are no guarantees when working with our children, because they have desires, minds, and wills of their own. Occasionally, in spite of everything that we do, some children end up making poor decisions, and a few lose their chastity. It is important in these situations to realize that all is not lost. There are many things we can do to help our children find their way back again.

To help us imagine how we would feel in this difficult situation, I have included some insights from a good Latter-day Saint couple who had to face this problem with one of their daughters. The couple was kind enough to share how they felt when they first found out that their daughter was pregnant and some of the feelings that followed during the next few weeks.

MOTHER: When the doctor came in and said that my daughter was pregnant, it still hit me real hard, even though

I thought that she might be. I was just numb, and I couldn't say anything. When we got into the car I started to cry, and I bawled all of the way home. My daughter was crying also, and we didn't say much. Finally I asked her, "Why didn't you tell me?" She said that she just couldn't. It was really hard! She felt really sorry at the time and, when we got home, she went right to her room and stayed in there and cried.

FATHER: Although I just knew that she was pregnant, the whole day while I was waiting, there was still that hope that I was wrong. I didn't want to accept it. When my wife told me that our daughter really was expecting, I quit work and started home. My feelings became worse and worse until I didn't want to face anyone. By the time I got home, there was no way I wanted to go into the house, because I was afraid of what I would do and say. So I simply started walking, and I walked for two or three miles. It was cold, and I didn't have a jacket on, but I didn't really care. I would just as soon have died. If I could have opened up a hole and crawled in and pulled the hole in over me, I would just as soon have done it. My daughter had turned against everything that I had ever taught her.

MOTHER: My husband handled it really well. I was proud of him. He walked and walked, and our daughter was afraid for him to come in and talk to her. When he finally came in, he had been thinking and praying. He came in, put his arms around her, and reassured her that he loved her and was disappointed that this had happened. I was really proud of him because I knew that he was upset and angry inside.

FATHER: If I had gone into the house right at first, I probably would have hit her, because that's what I really wanted to do. I wanted to take out my frustrations on her. It was hard for me when the boy came over to decide about the marriage. I found myself wanting to hit him when he stepped through the door.

MOTHER: We cried all night the first night, and it was hard for a long time to go to church and hear people bear their testimonies about their families and hear them talk about temple marriages that they had attended.

FATHER: My first reaction was to get them married and out of the house, and I struggled with these feelings for several days. I didn't want to speak with anyone, especially my friends and relatives. I was mad and thoroughly disgusted with everything, but talking to relatives and friends helped me get over these feelings.

MOTHER: We first thought that we would not give a nice reception but just a small open house. Everyone thought that we would lose them if we did and that they would never forgive us and be close to us. They told us that a nice reception would show them that we still loved them and build our relationship so that we could teach them. We really wanted that, but we felt very uncomfortable.

FATHER: I just couldn't figure out why. Why would she let her standards down? She had never given us any real problems.

MOTHER: We really felt like we had taught her chastity. We were constantly sharing ideas and concepts with her in an informal way. I kept telling her that she needed to have Heavenly Father's help when she dated and ought to pray before she went out on dates. I could feel her shutting me off, and I knew that she wasn't praying. That really worried me because I felt that she wasn't receiving the help that she needed from the Lord.

It was really worrying us that she wouldn't pray. When

she turned fifteen or sixteen her attitudes changed and she wanted to be popular. She didn't feel that it was the popular thing to be really religious. She didn't want to study the scriptures with us anymore and developed a poor attitude about having family home evening with us.

FATHER: You listen to your children pray when they are young and it's just a child's prayer. Her prayers had begun to mean something as she grew up. When she became fifteen, her prayers, instead of becoming better, started to go right back and become just words.

MOTHER: We really blamed ourselves. You can't help but blame yourself when this happens, and you're just devastated. We tried to do all the right things but somehow we failed. We failed!

FATHER: We thought, "Where did we go wrong? What did we do wrong?"

MOTHER: Maybe self-esteem? Maybe we didn't praise her enough and love her enough. We thought that we had, but we blamed ourselves anyway. I think that we feel better about it now, but at that time we really blamed ourselves. Everyone kept trying to tell us, "You can't blame yourselves—it happens to the best of families. All you can do is try to do your best."

FATHER: I had seen other people that had had these problems, and I could see that they didn't hold family home evening or that they were not very close to their kids. When it hit us, I just kept thinking, "What did we do wrong?" It was just really hard for me to accept. I think it was harder for me to accept than it was for my wife. I asked to be released from my Church position—how could I be an effective leader when I had failed with my daughter? The bishop refused to release me. Thank goodness for that.

MOTHER: We started to worry about our other children and what they would do with the gospel. If our one daughter did this, what would happen to them? It's still hard occasionally when parents talk about going to the temple with their children. When you have that goal for so many years and then this happens, it's hard.

These parents reacted as many of us would react under similar conditions. They did many things to help overcome the problem. Their comments reveal several important principles that can help any of us if we are faced with this problem. These principles are discussed below.

Review Past Conduct

We will feel better about things if we review the good things we have done in the past to help our children stay morally clean. These same things will also help our children repent. It is never too late to start doing these things with our children.

1. Study the scriptures and pray together.

2. Teach modesty and the facts of life and continue to discuss these areas openly and honestly.

3. Do fun things together as a family.

4. Support our children in their activities.

5. Hold personal interviews with our children.

6. Set an example in our choice of entertainment and reading material.

7. Spend lots of time with our children.

8. Express love in our speech and actions.

9. Listen to our children and respect their opinions.

10. Establish dating guidelines and standards consistent with the teachings of the Church.

Pray

The father of the girl who had been immoral took a walk and prayed before he approached his daughter. Our Father in heaven knows what our children need to hear, and it is critical that we pray and ask him for guidance and self-control before we approach a child with a moral problem. This will help us control our emotions and want to help the child rather than show our anger.

Show Love and Support

The couple in the example didn't criticize their daughter; they made every effort to show her that they still loved her. An extra effort needs to be made to demonstrate love, both in word and in deed.

Listen and Understand

Young people who have lost their chastity are faced with numerous emotional problems, and we need to let them know that we are concerned about *them*. Too many parents give the impression that they are more concerned with their own reputation than with the problems their teenagers are facing.

Only when we have come to understand how our teenagers feel are we in a position to offer much advice or direction. They could feel extremely sorry or not sorry at all. They may feel bad because they have lost their chastity, or they may feel bad because we have found out. They may feel repentant, or they may feel that there is no hope. We will never know how our children feel until we listen.

As we listen to our children, we cannot afford to act shocked, to criticize, or to stand in judgment. We must simply and honestly try to understand how they feel.

Help Them Determine Their Goals

After we have come to understand how our children feel, we might ask them, "What do you want to do now? What do you really want out of life?" Too many times we impose our own goals and wishes upon our children. We need to help them clarify what their future goals really are. They may then come to realize that they really do want the blessings of eternal life and the opportunities that the Church offers. They are then in a much better position to repent and do the things necessary to regain the Spirit and have full fellowship in the Church.

Help Them Repent

Once we know how our children feel and what they desire, we can advise them on what they need to do to repent. If they don't want to repent, we need to love them, pray for them, and stay close to them so that when they are ready we will be there.

Although children who have transgressed need to confess their sins to the bishop, we can help them realize that forgiveness comes from the Lord. The key to repentance is redeveloping a relationship with our Father in heaven and with Jesus Christ. This is done through prayer, study, and gospel living.

As they meet with the bishop, he may impose some restrictions on them. This is to help them realize the importance of chastity and the responsibilities that come with membership in the Church. They will need lots of love and support through this difficult period of their repentance. We can pray for them and with them and help them to repent.

Sometimes our children don't respond at the rate that we would like them to. Occasionally they don't seem to respond at all or even seem to retrogress in their relationship with us and the Lord. We need to patiently pray, show love, listen, try to understand, and look for ways to help them understand the gospel. Sometimes it takes years, but the Lord won't give up on them and neither should we. Most people cannot resist a spirit of love and concern over a long period of time.

We can't afford to be pushy. We need to give them room so they can grow without backing down or losing face. Most of our children will eventually respond and, if not, we need to keep in mind that each of us is responsible for his own actions and not blame ourselves for the decisions of our children. We will then be in a much better position to help them and others because we will feel good about ourselves and our relationship with the Lord.

Following are comments from teenagers about what parents can do when their children have been immoral:

1. *Love them! Show them that you care and want to help them. Don't shut them out. Keep in mind that the Lord still loves them and wants you to help them get back to him.*

2. *They have to try to become best friends and love each other so they can talk freely without feeling embarrassed and low.*

3. *Tell them that they will help them get their lives back together, and be on their side. Go to a counselor if they feel that their son or daughter needs it.*

4. *Show them that they still love and care about them and that they understand and want to help.*

5. *They should talk to them. They probably have problems and feel that their parents don't care about them. Parents should calmly talk to them and understand how they feel. They should let them know they care and want to help.*

6. *I think the best thing they can do is support them. I think that they should stand by them no matter what they have done. They also need to forgive and forget, not bringing it up all the time, because what is done is done.*

7. *Talk to them, let them know that they want to help them, and give them guidelines to repentance.*

8. *Try to understand their children and show that they really do care. Parents can explain not just that the children chose wrong but why it was wrong, and gradually lead them into the steps of repentance.*

9. *Forgive them, love them, still accept them. Try your best to trust them. Don't tell them what they should have done—they already know. Just be there so they have a shoulder to cry on.*

10. *Parents can understand and give their children as much love as possible. They can talk them into talking with the bishop and repenting.*

11. *Understand what they've done and not get mad at them. Direct them to the bishop but don't force them.*

12. *Talk to them and reassure them. Don't act like they are humiliated or embarrassed. Act like it is your problem too. Ask the children if they want to change. Maybe they don't! If they don't want to change, just let them go and keep praying for them.*

13. *Talk to them. Show them what they are doing with their lives. But don't be pushy, because young adults don't like pushy parents. They have to try to be as understanding as possible.*

14. *Not rush them, but not be real lenient about it either.*

15. *Let them know it isn't too late. They can become clean with time, but they must try really hard.*

16. *They can talk to them about what they did and why they did it and pray with them and help them talk to their bishop.*

17. *Don't smother them, but let them know that they still care about them. Let them know that they are not mad at them. Most of all, don't center everything around it.*

18. *Try to understand and don't get embarrassed or angry. Come closer to them instead of disowning them.*

Suggestions to Parents from Unwed Mothers

In this appendix, girls who have been pregnant out of wedlock respond to three questions: Why do some Latter-day Saint girls become pregnant out of wedlock? What can parents do to prevent their children from losing their chastity? What can the Church do to help teenagers stay morally clean?

Why Do Some Latter-day Saint Girls Become Pregnant Out of Wedlock?

1. *I was alone too much with my boyfriend, stayed out too late, and did too much necking and petting.*

2. *I didn't think I would get pregnant.*

3. *Everybody was doing it, so I was curious and thought I would try it too.*

4. *I wanted a temple marriage, but my testimony wasn't strong enough, and my commitment to my goals wasn't strong enough, so that when I was tempted and thought I loved the guy, I yielded.*

5. *I was trying to convert my boyfriend to the Church. His standards were different from mine and one night we got carried away.*

6. *I drank too much alcohol one night and couldn't re-member my values.*

7. *My boyfriend and I never wanted to go all the way. We just kept going further and further in sharing affection until we couldn't stop.*

8. *I wanted to get back at my father. He was a Church leader and felt that he was so righteous. He was always putting me down and telling me that I was no good. I knew that getting pregnant would hurt him.*

9. *I didn't get the love and affection that I needed at home, so I looked for it in the wrong way.*

10. *Sex seemed so glamorous in the movies and on TV. I thought it would be neat to try it.*

11. *I got pregnant before I knew how a girl gets pregnant.*

12. *My parents never talked to me about sex. No one told me what "going too far" was, and before I knew where to draw the line, I had gone too far. I still don't know where to draw the line.*

13. *I was part of the "ninety and nine" who were active, and when I told my bishop and others in the Church that I was having problems, they didn't take it seriously. They didn't worry about me because I was such a good girl.*

14. *I wasn't accepted by my peers at Church, so I found a group at school that would accept me, and they didn't have the same standards.*

15. *I was looking for love and security. I thought that I had to go "all the way" to keep my boyfriend.*

What Can Parents Do To Prevent Their Children from Losing Their Chastity?

1. *Sex education should be taught in the home. It should be discussed honestly and openly when a child asks questions, no matter the age. Parents should teach healthy attitudes toward sex and not that it's dirty or bad. Fathers should be involved in teaching their girls about sex as much as the mothers. Boys need to be taught that it is just as much their responsibility to stay morally clean as it is for the girls. Girls shouldn't always have to be the*

ones to say no. Sex should be taught on a spiritual level. Teens need to be taught clearly where to draw the line.

2. Parents need good communication with their children so that if they have a problem they can talk to them.

3. Children need physical affection in the home so they don't look for it in the wrong way.

4. Girls especially need a good relationship with their father so they won't desperately be looking for acceptance and love from a man and get in trouble.

5. If my parents hadn't been fighting all the time, maybe I would have felt more secure and not become pregnant.

6. My parents trusted me too much and didn't set limits. I wish they had told me what time I had to get home.

7. I needed more supervision by my parents when I was kissing my boyfriend in the family room.

8. My parents just told me what not to do and didn't give me any explanations so I would understand why. They didn't discuss practical issues about morality, like how to get out of a tempting situation if I was in one.

9. I wish my parents had taught me more about the Church so I would have had a stronger testimony and not been deceived.

10. My parents were always comparing me to my older brothers and sisters. I felt like I couldn't measure up, so I went the other way.

What Can the Church Do to Help Teenagers Stay Morally Clean?

1. Parents need to be taught how to teach their children about sex. How to teach children about sex should be taught in priesthood meeting as well as in Relief Society.

2. Families need to have family home evening lessons on sex and values.

3. Frank articles about sex and morality should be included in the New Era, the Ensign, and the Church News.

4. There should be more talks on morality by Church leaders in general conference or any other Church meetings.

5. Boys as well as girls need to be taught to be morally clean. They are just as responsible as the girls, even though they don't get pregnant.

6. Home teachers and visiting teachers should visit their people each month, especially if they are single adults living away from home. Even when I was inactive, it would have helped me to know that the Church still cared.

7. The Single Adult program needs to teach service instead of having mainly self-centered, social activities.

8. We need more guidance from the bishops on how to repent when we've made a mistake. They assume we know what to do even though that may not be the case.